Debate
Craves Conflict

A key to the best social media engagement

Sharon Lina Pearce

the author of Better Learning Communities

Twitter: @sharonlinapearc
www.sharonlinapearce.com
Blog: www.betterlearningcommunities.com
Book: http://tiny.cc/BuildABetterLearningComm

DEDICATION

This book is dedicated to all Community Managers and Social Media Managers who constantly strive to raise the mark by learning, creating, experimenting and implementing.

@sharonlinapearc

CONTENTS

RE-MASTERING POSTS

An explanation

My blog posts are created as topics trend, as questions arise or as solutions are needed to an obstacle I am confronting. As such, my blog posts do not tell a story from beginning to end in the order published.

This quick guide is a reordering of some of these posts; focusing on my community planning and content building process, which will arrange the concepts so that subsequent posts build upon the previous ones.

They are also re-mastered, by which I mean rewritten, so that the posts, as a unit, now tell a story and provide community managers with ideas when planning to engage and interact an online community.

When changes are needed for clarity, the original Better Learning Community post will be modified.

HARBOR DEBATE

CONFLICT AND LOCATION

It can be hard to get a discussion going online. Where you create a discussion thread and how you create it make the difference in the amount of interaction generated.

Debates crave conflict because the latter incites strong emotion thus leading to engagement of opposing views. Managed debates around conflict can lead to greater understanding and learning.

Discussions and debates, even virtual ones, need to take place somewhere. So, I have included three blog posts which define how to create the virtual space where these conversations will take place, among whom and how to encourage participants to come back to debate some more.

1. DEFINE THE COMMUNITY

Imagine what members can contribute to this community.

Yesterday, I was asked how to create an **interactive community**.

The person asking was wondering what to consider before setting it up, how to anticipate the intended public's needs and how to pick a name. Here is the outline that I sent her.

"Creating a Community" Worksheet

- Why did you create this community?
- Who are your supporters and experts?
- How will this community benefit the target group?
- What should individual members derive from this community?
- Imagine what members can contribute to this community:

- What type of resources are you, as a CM, planning to provide for your community?
- Extract key words from the above description.
- Based on the key words, create the name of your group

Original Title: *Define Your New Community Worksheet*

This blog post was the basis for the Planning section of my book, *How to Build Better Learning Communities*; tiny.cc/BuildABetterLearningComm.

2. DESIGN THE LANDING PAGE

Do you see any activities that you can do?
Can you see the latest content?

Let's determine if the landing page you've created for your **community is viable**. Pretend you have never visited your landing page. Go there and determine of you see any of the following <u>without</u> scrolling down:
1. Do you see any activities that you can do?
2. Can you see the latest content?
3. Do the links drive you further into the community or somewhere else?
4. Is there an obvious way to join, follow or subscribe to a newsletter?

If you do not see these items, consider redesigning your landing page following the viability list:
1. Activities engage visitors and make them stay longer.

2. If a visitor does not see recent content, they might conclude that no one is talking here or that the place isn't trending and there is no perceived value.
3. Try to design the landing page so that the visitor stays longer and interacts more. Place links that drive your audience into your community at the top. If you must post links to other places...move it on down the page!
4. The visitor may not find your community again or remember to come back. To invite the visitor back with an invitation or a newsletter, make it easy for the visitor to register.

With this said, I am going to post an example which I created for my upcoming eBook, "How to Build Better Learning Communities", which (*when I wrote this blog post*) is still in draft. I am not going to cheat. I am posting it exactly as I have it designed for the book. Does it meet my own test or will I have to revise it for my book?

Answers for the Stronger Sales Team landing page

1. Activities? Yes, I can vote, participate in discussions and listen to a webinar.
2. Latest Content? Yes, I can see it located front and center
3. Links into the community? I see that ninety percent of the links drive me further into the community. However, the first item under "The Latest in Our Community" will eventually leads me out but first goes to an internal summary page. The learning links under "Learn with Experts" link out to some type of learning platform but it is at the bottom right.
4. An easy way to register? Yes, and there is a bonus. As a new member, I get profiled in the new member box.

It appears that the landing page I designed passed my own test! Please put yours to the test too.

Original Title: *Does Your Landing Page Send People Away*

This blog post was originally written to organize my own thoughts on the subject of retention of new users and is included in *How to Build Better Learning Communities*; tiny.cc/BuildABetterLearningComm.

3. REACH THE RIGHT AUDIENCE

For each group, emphasize the community content and activities which are of greatest interest for employees in those areas.

Establishing **who you wan**t to or need to attract to your **community** is critical. Why waste effort trying to contact and recruit the wrong people?

To determine who needs to be contacted and how to market to them, let's review the different <u>types of audiences</u> which are typically the focus of learning; the entire company, a specific population or unidentified people distributed around the company.

The Entire Company

Safety training applies to everyone. Company-wide training initiatives enjoy backing from company execs. It is easy to initially contact the entire group via a company-wide, exec-signed email pointing people to the community that houses it.

Promote the community by communicating with your

target audience's managers. Tell the managers more about the learning initiative, how to get to the community and how learning continues there and the benefits of coming back. Ask the managers to pass on the information to their people verbally; in meetings or during an all-hands session.

A Specific Population
When a specific population, such as people managers, is defined for learning; identification of the group is nothing more than a call to Human Resources.

To personalize your message for subsets of your target audience, find out who the people managers for engineering are as well as for sales or for general services. For each group, emphasize the community content and activities which are of greatest interest for employees in those areas.

Unidentified People Distributed
This target audience is a marketing challenge for the learning community owner. Your potential audience is everyone in the company but the real audience is but a small percentage of the whole. If you are running a learning community about a specific subject; e.g., Marketing & Communications, you will need to attract the audience which has need of company icons, presentations.

1. Establish an ad and a permanent link from the Marketing Intranet page. Invite the first people to join the community to become special supporters or volunteers. Recognize their contribution by listing them as co-owners or advocates in your learning community or adding a contributor's badge to their profile page.
2. Several departments are obvious consumers of these types of materials. Invite the members of each of these departments to a chat about the community. Make it optional so that only people with an interest attend. A demo of the learning community asking attendees to sign on and interact with the community is the most effective.
3. A monthly newsletter pushes out key items to interested users. Post a 'Subscribe to the Newsletter' link in the Marketing Intranet and combine that list with the people who join your community to create a mailing list. Ask the recipients to pass the newsletter on to other interested co-workers.

Original Title: *Find Your Audience and Reach Out to Them*

This blog post served as an inspiration for obtaining new users and is discussed in *How to Build Better Learning Communities*; tiny.cc/BuildABetterLearningComm.

INCREASE DEBATE

CONFLICT AND CONTENT

This is the rasion d' être of putting this work together.

So many attempts of starting a conversation online fail.
One reason is the way the subject or content is presented.
Even if the initial content has potential, the audience never
even reads it.

To increase engagement, there are a couple of basic rules
to content in an online community
1. Pique the potential audience's curiosity
2. Entice the reader with glimpses of the content
3. Challenge your audience to respond

4. THE RIGHT CONTENT

If a member of a group needs to work on their listening skills, a thread about the issue would invite all parties to discuss it.

What is the right content for your learning community? Relevant content, of course, and let's not forget engaging! Be it polls or debates about great courses or the subject du jour, any content which draws members in is the right content.

Does that mean that fun content can be appropriate for a community post? We discussed this in a thread the other day and I said, "Not only is it appropriate but necessary!"

Fun content can address conflict
Take a look at this Dilbert comic strip (http://dilbert.com/strip/2010-12-24). This is fun content but it also instructs us on how important good listening is to a conversation. This would be relevant for a learning community which addresses softskills or communications. No, not relevant; perfect.

Members will laugh at it and either remember someone they know who is like Dogbert or wonder if they sometimes commit similar errors. Ah, food for thought and reflection.

Imagine this comic strip as a header to an anonymous poll entitled, "Know Anyone Who Listens Worse than Dogbert?" with the following options:

- Yes, at work
- Yes, at my last job
- Yes, at home!
- Yes, I do that sometimes
- No, thank goodness I don't

If a member of a community needs to work on their listening skills, a thread about the issue would invite all parties to discuss it. Consider a slightly antagonistic title. Encourage everyone to participate in the thread; including the guilty party.

Bonus: Fun content is also a marketing tool

Putting a smile on someone's face is a sure fire way of getting them to return to your community and participate in more conversations. Fun content is the way to create a smile and fun can be found in many places; a comic strip, a video of a cute baby doing something bad, a quote that summarizes a situation or a great story.

In a realtor's community, I read the fun story about the Queen of England revoking the US' independence and the subsequent changes her new subjects would suffer. The realtor used this as her principal story rather than a dry story about buying and selling houses (although this information could be found as well). The centerpiece for her community was funny. Fun is her catch and is the reason people return to that community.

Yes, fun content is the right content for your learning community. Enjoy it!

Original Title: *Is Fun Content Right for Your Community?*

This blog post launched my blog, www.betterlearningcommunities.com. This is when I realized that much of what I had learned was of use to others who were starting similar journeys.

5. WRITING IT RIGHT

No one created a conversation.

Yesterday, I posted in an online communications group. I titled the post, "Why Do You Discourage Others?" and referenced an article that I had read in BBC news about a runner being heckled. Then, I asked readers if they had ever discouraged others or been discouraged by others and how they handled situation.

Dead Battery Syndrome
After publishing, I looked down the list of other posts on the site. I was disappointed to see that they were not garnering responses. I thought I had posted to an active group! What was happening here? Were members not interested in engaging? Were the posts not motivating them to respond? I examined the posts more closely and found:
- One told others about a great article that they should read
- Another wanted to know if anyone had read the latest sales presentation

- And a photo of a piece of equipment

No one remembered to ask a leading question to engage the audience. No one took sides on an issue. No one challenged readers to respond. No one created a conversation.

With Jumper Cables

Imagine you post a great article and mention several co-workers so they will read it. Do they just scan the article and leave it for later? To get a response and encourage interaction:

- Create a discussion title which is a question. It implies that you value their opinion. Provocative questions make readers feel passionately about their opinion.
- Make it a 'Why' or 'How' question. This helps them understand that they are helping you gain insight on an issue.
- Tell them you need their thoughts by 3pm in order to prepare a presentation. This increases the likelihood that they will read the article, look at other's comments & respond.

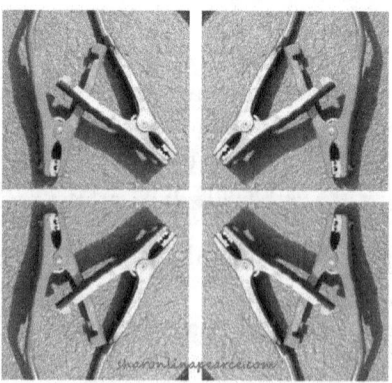

Original Title: *Know How to Jump-start Conversation?*

This blog post was written due to my surprise that so much content existed that did not invite the reader to converse. The blog post was the inspiration for writing this short reference booklet.

6. POWERFUL QUESTIONS

Remember, you want to create a minor conflict, not a war.

This is a list of my favorite types of questions which make readers react. These are my designations from observing what does and does not make members of enterprise social learning groups react.

Make 'em Choose Sides. This is a question type I use when I want members to analyze an item or understand a subject in greater depth. But remember, you want to create a minor conflict, not a war.

Pick a question that won't offend a group or invite radical responses. For a group studying social media, this easy question will get Twitter users of all levels of experience talking, *"Twitter-quette; is saying thank-you unnecessary or a must do?"*

What I find difficult about creating this type of question is avoiding a yes-no question. A lot of my great ideas pop into my head as yes-no questions. I write them down and do several re-writes until I get the format that will make the reader choose sides. This is what gets the conversation going and makes them explore the subject matter.

Ask Them How.
Let members coach one another by asking them to share their experiences and best practices. This type of question asks readers to reveal how they approached and solved a problem. The more you know your audience, the easier it is to create a question which one of your readers has the experience to answer.

One example of this type of question is, "What communication tools did you use in your virtual team?" which really asks them how they communicate.

Make the question unrestrictive so that many people have a chance of contributing and sharing their experiences.

When I originally drafted this question, I wrote, "Ever **led** a virtual team? What tools did you use to communicate?" The first question solicits a yes-no answer and the question is exclusive. Fewer people have led virtual teams while a lot of people have worked on a virtual team. Anyone on a virtual team knows the tools used and how effective they were.

Original Title: *Powerful Questions for You to Use*

This blog post was based on analysis of my personal experience and added input for the Content section of *How to Build Better Learning Communities*; tiny.cc/BuildABetterLearningComm.

7. BETTER ENGAGEMENT

By challenging one of the conclusions of the article, I set the stage for disagreement...

In a previous post, I talked about leading title questions to jump-start conversation encouraging readers to click into a discussion. In this post, let's ensure that readers:

- Digest that content
- Reply to that content

Comprehension depends on my abilities as a communicator

When I open a discussion and find a request to read a three-page article and respond, I don't read it. I do not have the time especially if the subject isn't directly related to my work. I checked to see how co-workers responded in similar situations and found that their reaction was quite similar to mine.

So, I devised a two-layer solution that makes content easy to consume. When referencing an article, I link to that article *and*:

- I briefly explain why the audience should read it
- I summarize the take-away points.
- I challenge the audience to disagree with one of the points in the article

The audience can read my summary. If they want to know more, they can click on the article link. By giving the audience two choices, I have increased the possible number of discussion responders. By challenging one of the conclusions of the article, I set the stage for disagreement letting readers decide if I am right or wrong and why.

Readers will reply if I ask the right question
I review content and title compatibility at this point. Do they support each other? Is the question asking the reader to react? Did I ask the audience to choose sides or share their experience? Does it encourage the reader to write back?

Other Hints

- Double check that you are publishing where your subject will be of interest
- Use bullet points for quick reading of the main take-away points
- Use imagery to get their attention
- Make your title @mentionable in another entry; i.e., in a sentence. Does everyone Know How to Jump-start Conversation?

Original Title: *Want Conversations or Discussion DOA?*

This blog post was created to share with community members wanting to create conversations online and builds on the Content section of *How to Build Better Learning Communities*; tiny.cc/BuildABetterLearningComm.

8. KEEP ARGUING

*There is nothing easier than **disagreeing** with the previous answer to entice others to join your side or the other side of the discussion.*

Keeping a discussion going helps community members to interact with each other. It helps them explore on a deeper level if you make them analyze the topic, defend their position and look for supporting materials for their arguments. There is no better way to learn! This form of learning energizes me and I walk away with a greater understanding of the topic every time.

The easiest way to keep a discussion going is to **answer the question** yourself if the uptake is slow in the community. Offer a partial answer or just start mulling the discussion question over and avoid giving an authoritative answer as it will stop the discussion.

You can @mention someone whom you think would know more about the topic; an **advocate or expert** thus inviting yet another person to the discussion.

There is nothing easier than **disagreeing** with the previous answer to entice others to join your side or the other side of the discussion. If a reply states that Mandarin is the more widely spoken than Cantonese, reply that you think that Cantonese is more widely spoken because the provinces where it is spoken are more populous. Let the discussion ensue as learners disagree with you!

Present **other points of view** broadening the scope of the conversation. A discussion about feeling confident before a presentation will include a few hints. Add another hint and tell a story about how it helped you once.

Original Title: *Keep the Discussion Going*

This blog post illustrates ways of keeping valuable discussions active in the community and added to the Content section of *How to Build Better Learning Communities*; tiny.cc/BuildABetterLearningComm.

9. LET IT GO

All discussions must come to an end

For November, I succumb to temptation and write a Halloween-themed piece about dead discussions. All discussions must come to an end. Even discussions are full of lively opinions will eventually wilt and die. Rather than just leaving the discussion for dead, why not bury it?

Why Bury It
Not all discussions need a burial but those which contributed to the knowledge base, added resources or innovative points of view deserve a send-off so that they can be remembered – or at least the most important points that they made can be remembered.

When to Leave it for Dead & How to Bury It

Discussions reach a point where there is no more to learn from them and the participants have pretty much talked the subject out.

After 10 days of practicing irregular plurals in a language community, most basics have been covered. There are only so many irregular plural nouns; even in English. Leave the participants with one last entry in the language discussion which helps them keep learning; perhaps a reference to an Internet page which lists all the irregular plurals and has interactive exercises.

Tacit knowledge exchange about a single subject has an upper limit too. As the sales team debates the many benefits that effective listening can bring to the sales process, most of the options are explored and interest dies down. Give the discussion the send off it deserves by creating a resource out of the success stories discussed.

When a topic is no longer timely; such as an organizational change announcement, there is no further need for constant chatter about the information. Close out this type of discussion with a way for people to contact those named in the announcement.

Original Title: *Burying Dead Discussions*

This blog post reminds us that there is a natural end to conversations. This post helped me define the value of interaction in learning content which is reflected in *How to Build Better Learning Communities*; tiny.cc/BuildABetterLearningComm.

MORE INTERACTION
Excerpt from "How to Build Better Learning Communities"

By the reports which we see on activity in our community, there is a very satisfactory level of content 'views' but the amount of interaction is low. The average number of responses to discussions is five and, often times, the same group of people are involved in the various discussions. We would like to see a wider range of people interact enhancing the amount of tacit knowledge exchanged. Our action plan:

- Ensure that members know how to interact by providing simple documentation, making it easy to find online and pushing it out to our members.
- Create 'quick-reply' content; i.e. content which does not require more than 2 minutes of their time to read, digest and respond. This could be in the form of polls or light discussions which do not reference reading material.
- Personally reach out to the newest members and

ask them for their opinion on a piece of content. The benefit to this exercise is the discovery of what they need to get started.

- Complement the newsletter push marketing with another type of occasional push marketing such as an announcement or an email highlighting a specific piece of content.

To increase interaction, create 'quick-reply' content; i.e., content which does not require more than 2 minutes to read, digest and respond.

O. To Increase Responses

#Content #Member Training

Original Title: *10 Apr - Pushing for More Interaction*

This chapter from my book looks at brevity in content and diversity of people which naturally leads to increased interaction, divergent opinions and debate.

How to Build Better Learning Communities; tiny.cc/BuildABetterLearningComm.

SOURCES OF CONFLICT, I MEAN, CONTENT
A reference

During this economic downturn budgets have been cut for a lot of things including training. One of the less expensive training options I created to meet tighter budget constraints was a social learning site to provide no-cost learning resources for both technical skills and softskills.

Finding no-cost content which is reliable can prove challenging. I found the challenge greater for technical training (in which my knowledge is more limited) then for English language training. I looked both within the company and within the marketplace to locate good sources. I find these types of sites to have the greatest potential to provide training at no additional cost to the learner or the company.

First, look closely at any **internal** resources if this is an enterprise site. Don't just look once but rather keep your eyes continuously open as the real gems will slowly appear as you become more involved.

- Internal newsletters on the subject
- Toolboxes on the corporate Intranet
- Related videos posted on the company web
- Any type of Learning Management System or online course portal
- Company-wide or subject matter databases
- Specialized groups on your internal social network

Then, consider external **Internet** resources such as:
- Companies working in the field (Cisco, ALU)
- Established authorities (HBR)
- Government agencies (NIST)
- Industry rags or Tech mags (Global Cellular,
- Newspapers and media companies (BBC)
- Professional Social Networks (LinkedIn)
- Universities (Johns Hopkins)
- Working groups or Not-for-Profits (.org)

Original Title: *No-Cost Learning Content.*

This blog post is valuable to a community manager who looks for trending topics to feed to the community. This post is the cornerstone for finding content sources in *How to Build Better Learning Communities*; tiny.cc/BuildABetterLearningComm.

ABOUT THE AUTHOR

Sharon Lina Pearce is an eternal student of communities and everything that makes them a source of interaction, education and development.

She uses social for her own continuing education as well as for networking, collaborating, marketing, outreach and education of others in both her personal and professional life.

Twitter: @sharonlinapearc
www.sharonlinapearce.com
www.betterlearningcommunities.com
http://tiny.cc/BuildABetterLearningComm

www.ingramcontent.com/pod-product-compliance
Lightning Source LLC
Chambersburg PA
CBHW071553170526
45166CB00004B/1657